HOW TO HIRE A NANNY

HOW TO HIRE A NANNY

A Complete Step By Step Guide For Parents

Elaine S. Pelletier

André and Lanier, Denver, Colorado

Published by:
André & Lanier
6860 S. Yosemite Court, Suite 200
Englewood, Colorado 80112

Cover design by:
Graphic Directions & Advertising, Inc.
Boulder, Colorado

Printed in the United States of America

Publisher's Cataloging in Publication Data

       Pelletier, Elaine S.
       How To Hire A Nanny, A Complete Step By Step Guide
           For Parents
       1. Parenting,   2. Child Care
       ISBN   0-9635575-7-2
       LC 93-0072335

All names of persons, street addresses and phone numbers herein are part of an entirely fictitious scenario or scenarios and are designed solely for clarification or demonstration purposes.

For my parents,
with
love and admiration
always

My greatest appreciation to the following people who generously contributed their experience, ability, and enthusiasm to this project:

Barbara Dignan
Pete Dignan
Dr. Dan Eicher
Mary Eicher
Dr. Daniel J. Feiten
Genie Fellmer
Glenn Gillette
Jeanne Gillette
Ralph Hubregsen
Karen Keefe
Dr. Sue Moison
André J. Pelletier
Theresé Pelletier
Karen Sutherland
Sue Teague
Sarah Tracy
Rosann B. Ward

Special thanks to Jennifer, Emily, and Roger Kobylarczyk.

CONTENTS

From The Author 1

Introduction 3

Defining the Job 6

- What's Important to You? 6
- Fundamental Issues 8
- Practical Matters 12
- Writing a Job Description 18

Tasks & Responsibilities Worksheet
Job Description

The Cost of In-home Care 30

- Peace Of Mind 31
- How Much Should I Pay? 32
- Salary Versus Hourly Wages 33
- Benefits 35
- Becoming An Employer 37

What To Do/When To Do It

Finding the Right Nanny 45

- Using An Agency 46
- Timing 48
- Advertising And Networking 49
- Interviewing - Helpful Hints 52
- Reach Out And Touch Someone 53

Finding the Right Nanny (continued)

- References 63
- Up Close And Personal 69
- Making A Selection 71
- Extending An Offer 77

> *Phone Interview*
> *Reference Questionnaire*
> *Job Description Cover Letter*
> *Employment Application*
> *Offer Letter*

Manage With Care **81**

- Getting Started 81
- Talk, Talk, Talk 84
- Growing Pains And Gains 86

Changes For The Better **90**

- When Family Priorities Change 90
- When Things Aren't Working Out 91

Afterthoughts **95**

FROM THE AUTHOR

I am a business professional, wife, and mother of two young children. If I ever thought about being a superwoman — you know, doing it all, having it all — it was only a fleeting fantasy born in a moment of self-delusion. I've never met one of these super beings. In fact, I'm convinced they exist only in contemporary mythology — like no-run panty hose and social security.

I am, however, well adjusted and content with my selection of life roles. Any given moment may bring harmony or conflict, but when viewed apart from the daily trials and tribulations, I enjoy a productive career, a happy family, and a strong marriage. (Okay, so I can't stay up past 9:30 most nights, and I know more about Big Bird than the President — but this is a small price to pay!)

I know many women and men who would describe their life as I have. While our priorities or roles may vary, we strive for balance and are rewarded with satisfaction in our business and families. We each have our formulas for keeping it all together, and invariably, child care is a big part of the equation.

That is why I have written this Guide. It's a combination of my own personal experience and insights I have gained from other parents.   The intended benefit of the Guide is to provide information about hiring a nanny in a single complete source. Included are short cuts to getting organized (check lists and questionnaires, for example) and recommendations to improve the efficiency of your search and quality of care once you have hired a nanny.

As you read, you will find that most of the information is straight-forward common sense — the child psychologists and talk show hosts are your best bet if you are looking for the true meaning of parenthood. That doesn't mean you won't discover some new ideas or approaches within this Guide! The point is to provide a useful, simple resource for practical-minded people. Life is hectic enough and let's face it: you don't want to spend your life reading about nannies — you want to get one hired!

It is my sincerest hope that you will benefit from the experience reflected in the following pages.   So, congratulations on your parenthood (especially if it's a recent blessing) and good luck from a fellow parent!

INTRODUCTION

When you welcome a child into your family, you embark on one of life's most fulfilling journeys. Your journey begins with incredulous wonder at the strength and beauty of this new life. Soon, this sense of wonder is joined by anxieties of all shapes and sizes as you realize the enormity of your responsibility. For in parenthood, overwhelming wonder, anxiety, and love are among the many incredible emotions which become lifelong companions.

There are also many practical aspects of parenting. Some things do come 'naturally' (a huge relief if you worried, like most new parents, about whether there really is such a thing as maternal instinct). Other things we learn with the help of friends and family who have 'been there' before us. In many ways, the experience of being a parent hasn't changed for many generations and thankfully so. There is, however, one aspect that has changed for today's parents and that can pose a significant challenge. This is the practical reality of child care.

For most of our parents, and certainly for theirs before them, the concept of child care by a non-family member didn't exist. The traditional family structure held few options other than Dad as the breadwinner and Mom as the housewife. Today's contemporary family structures offer greater freedom of choice for everyone. As a result, our generation is learning to balance individual choices for Mom and Dad with the well-being of the family as a whole. Child care is a critical element of this balancing act and often prompts a re-evaluation of choices and priorities.

Jobs, careers, hobbies, sports, friends — how do they compare to baby's first smile? first steps? first school play? The business trip that used to be an interesting diversion is now filled with heartache, hourly phone calls cooing to your three-month-old, and a suitcase full of pictures! And, for many, there is often a nagging guilt that you and only you can raise your child.

Well it's true — you *are* the only one who can make the difficult choices and sacrifices necessary to raise your child. It is also true that today's parents are successfully exercising both traditional and contemporary options for child care. They have recognized that being 'on location' full time is not the same as being one hundred percent involved and committed to your child and your family's well-being. These parents are successful because they pledge their full commitment and involvement to the task of selecting and maintaining quality child care.

Quality child care comes in many forms, each with different advantages and drawbacks requiring your careful consideration. Although you may feel very clear on your preferences, it is worthwhile to talk with child care providers (of all varieties) and other parents to gain additional insights into each option. You can also check with your local library or bookstore for other guides and publications if you have not completed your evaluation of child care options.

It's normal to experience conflicting emotions as you sort through this important decision. However, if you take the time to become fully educated, acknowledge your limitations, and remain committed to your priorities, you will make a decision with confidence.

About This Guide

Once you have determined the kind of child care you desire, the process of selecting a caregiver can be almost as overwhelming, especially to new parents. This Guide is intended to assist those families who have selected child care in the form of a live-out nanny.

For the purposes of clarification, a live-out nanny is someone who comes to your home on a regular schedule to provide care for your children exclusively. Although 'in-home' can refer to a situation where your child is cared for in someone else's home (rather than an institutional or corporate day care center), the term 'in-home' is used throughout this Guide to mean in *your* home.

While in-home care offers many excellent advantages, a typical concern is the cost and difficulty in finding a qualified nanny. In this Guide, you will find a common sense approach with explanations, examples, and reference information for hiring and working with your live-out nanny.

The Guide is organized into several main topics. This format allows you to read the entire guide or select individual topics as you require.

Throughout you will likely note a tendency for a consistent gender reference for a parent ('mother'), child ('him') and nanny ('her'). This is done strictly for ease of explanation and is not intended to imply a gender bias for a particular role. In any instance, feel free to substitute the alternate gender equally!

DEFINING THE JOB

In-home child care is appealing to many parents due to the benefits of keeping your child in his own family environment. Whether he is with you or with his nanny, all the goodness of his own home — toys, daily schedule and routine, playmates — become a consistent part of his care and well being. It follows then, that your nanny will become an integral part of your home and family, and it is with this in mind that you must define her role.

What's Important to You?

The process of hiring the ideal nanny starts with a clear definition of her role as it relates to you and your family. For example, some families emphasize cleanliness over all else. Others consider the television to be the downfall of civilization as we know it. Parenthood is uniquely personal too. What may be completely obvious to you isn't even in the realm of possibility for the next parent. Begin by taking the time to understand your family values, priorities and limitations.

Here are a few considerations to keep in mind as you develop your priorities:

• Be sure to include the whole family in this process. In some instances, this may mean getting input from step-children or in-laws. Everyone's participation up front will foster a positive, receptive attitude towards the nanny.

• Resist the urge to set aside your own personal needs in favor of focusing exclusively on your child. If exercise is an important part of your day, consider adjusting your nanny's hours to accommodate your visits to the gym.

• Consider how you can establish a foundation of mutual respect and courtesy between you and your nanny right from the start. As she becomes integrated into your family, you will also become a major factor in her life. Don't forget that she is a person with feelings and interests. If you define her role with this in mind, it will help you develop a job description which encourages a workable combination of her role as employee and family member.

• It's best to define her role as an extension of your parenting style, rather than as a substitute for your own perceived parental short comings. Here's a difficult situation: you live on junk food, but want to emphasize healthy eating habits for your child. You insist that your nanny offer strictly nutritional meals but you invariably give in to your own bad habits when you're in charge. This approach creates frustration for everyone.

The answer is obviously not to hire a junk-food addict for a nanny! The best advice is to proceed with the conviction that your children will always follow what you do, rather than what you say (or tell your nanny).

Fundamental Issues

Most parents will agree on these basic priorities for a nanny. These apply regardless of the age or number of children under her care:

- *Safety*

Your nanny must be diligent in matters of safety for your child. Do you want to restrict your nanny from driving with your child? Do you want to require a CPR certificate? Will you permit activities, such as swimming, which could pose a risk?

- *Health*

Your nanny will be responsible for routine health issues including nutrition and physical well being. Will she be preparing your child's daily menu or will you select meals? How do you want her to handle minor ailments, for example, a cold or slight fever? Should she administer medication or consult you first?

- *Happiness*

In addition to a healthy, safe environment, you want to ensure that your child is happy and well adjusted with your child care choices. This is best accomplished by selecting a nanny who is caring and enthusiastic about her role in your child's life. A nanny who has chosen this role because she truly loves children will be a valuable source of insight to your child and will influence his environment for the better.

Think about how you will select and work with a nanny based upon your family's priorities and needs. The following is a list of issues which tend to vary in importance from family to family.

- *Finances*

Money problems are considered among the highest potential sources of conflict within a family. Therefore, it is critical to understand how a nanny will impact your budget. If her salary will require cutbacks or sacrifices, be sure you are comfortable with your choices. You cannot establish a positive environment for your child if it is fraught with tension or resentment.

- *Religion*

If religious beliefs have an important role in your family, you may want to consider a nanny who shares your faith or a similar one. This will enable her to influence your child's development in a fashion which is consistent with your beliefs. On the other hand, some families value exposure to different faiths and will welcome a diverse influence for their child.

- *Culture*

In many ways this is similar to religion in that some families prefer sameness, while others value differences. In either case, consider culture as an opportunity to enrich your child's environment and select a candidate you are comfortable with.

✗ - *Discipline*

Some parents know exactly how and when they will discipline their children — even before they have them! Other parents have an evolving style based a variety of factors: the child's personality or age, their parent's style, or their pediatrician's advice. Whatever your style, you must find an effective way to communicate it to your nanny because consistency is very important for you and your child in matters of discipline.

How do you feel about spanking or physical discipline? Do you make a distinction between discipline (correcting a child's behavior) and punishment (penalizing a child for inappropriate behavior) — and should your nanny be empowered to administer both? Do you classify offenses and the associated disciplinary response? For example, a time-out is automatic and mandatory if your two-year-old plays with the dog's food (an invitation to a dog bite!). On the other hand, a time-out is optional for other lesser infractions.

'Time-out' is a popular practice for parents using child care. Most day care institutions use a combination of Redirection and Time-out theory to handle inappropriate behavior. Redirection helps the child focus on a more acceptable behavior and is positive, rather than negative, reinforcement. A time-out physically removes the child from a problem situation to a neutral space without any negative interaction.

Another technique associates poor behavior with the elimination of favorite activities or possessions (i.e., "if you can't control your temper this morning, we won't go to the park for lunch"). ✷This approach is positive for both your nanny and your child. Your nanny can work within her areas of influence to foster good behavior. Your child gains self-esteem as he learns that he is responsible for his behavior and the associated consequences.

As you can see, there are many things to consider on the issue of discipline. If you can anticipate your requirements and preferences in this area, you will be more likely to hire a nanny who will meet your needs.

- *Entertainment/Education*

Do you expect your 18-month-old to speak French fluently as a second language? Perhaps he should be able to name all the characters on Sesame Street? Think about any goals or rules for entertainment and educational activities you have that your nanny will need to support.

✗ Do you have a preference or concern about activities outside your home? Do you want to encourage trips to the zoo, library, museum — or are you uncomfortable with that much traveling around? These are considerations you'll want to explore with potential candidates up front.

A clear advantage of an in-home nanny is your ability to direct the educational opportunities available to your child each day. If this is a high priority for you, consider writing a daily or weekly activity plan for your child and his nanny. The plan can be as simple as a diary or calendar. It should identify regular activities you expect to be accomplished (reading, doing art projects, playing a musical instrument, etc.) as well as special events to attend (museum exhibits or the children's theater, for example). The nanny you select should be enthusiastic about this approach to education and fun for your child.

- *Communication*

Some parents feel comfortable with an open exchange of ideas about their child, while others prefer minimal input from their nanny. Of course you want regular feedback on daily events and activities, but do you want to encourage an open exchange of ideas on all topics? How will you handle the following situation: you think it's time to potty train, but your nanny doesn't?

Your ability to communicate effectively with your nanny is key to achieving your goals for quality care.

Your expectations of a nanny will take shape as you discuss and prioritize these issues. This effort will help you complete a personalized check list for evaluating candidates. You may even decide to include some of these issues as discussion points in your interview process.

Practical Matters

Once you have reviewed the fundamentals, you'll want to consider the more practical matters of the job. The scope of responsibilities for a live-out nanny varies dramatically from one family to another. Similarly, perceptions about the job are different from one nanny to another. Some candidates will be insulted by a request for housework, while others consider it a given.

Make the care of your child the top priority as you compose your list of responsibilities for your nanny. Know where you will and will not compromise for the sake of a particular candidate.

The following is a comprehensive list of tasks and responsibilities which are typical for a live-out nanny. Keep in mind that some items are specific to certain age groups and may become a requirement, or be eliminated as a requirement, over time.

Use this list as a worksheet to select those responsibilities which are important to you. The right side is intentionally left blank for your own notes. This list is also a good start for your Job Description, which is discussed in the following section.

Responsibilities	Notes
Direct Supervision	
Planning Activities • inside • outside • field trips	
Meals & Snacks • planning menus • preparing food • nutritional requirements	
Dressing	
Bathing/Cleanliness	
Supporting Developmental Activities • motor skills • social skills • eating skills • potty training	

TASKS & RESPONSIBILITIES

Responsibilities	Notes
Supporting Family Chores • enforcing responsibilities	
Imparting Discipline	
Minding Manners	
Health • going to the doctor • administering medicine • sick days (for your child)	
Teaching	
Friends/Neighbors • playing at your house • playing at their house	
Other	

TASKS & RESPONSIBILITIES

Schedule	Notes
Start of the day routine	

Meals
 	
   • breakfast
   • lunch
   • dinner
   • snacks	

Naps
 	
   • morning
   • afternoon	

End of the day routine	

Exceptions:
 	
   • holidays
   • partial days
   • evenings
   • weekends
   • sick days
   • vacations	

TASKS & RESPONSIBILITIES

Housekeeping	Notes
Picking up the house: • toys • play areas • yard	
Picking up your child's room: • making bed • closet • clothes	
Laundry: • your child's laundry • household laundry • family laundry	
Cleaning: • dusting • vacuuming • kitchen • bath rooms	

TASKS & RESPONSIBILITIES

Errands & Other	Notes
Grocery Shopping	
Running Errands	
Transportation: • to day care or school • to activities/lessons	
Watering Plants	
Preparing Family Meals	
Caring For Pets	
Cooking	
Other	

TASKS & RESPONSIBILITIES

Writing a Job Description

The next step in defining the job is writing the Job Description. The Job Description should reflect your priorities for a live-out nanny and can be general or specific, depending on your preference. You should clearly state your requirements so you and candidates can make realistic decisions and commitments.

The Job Description has a number of uses:

- You will use it throughout the interview process to qualify candidates and, when appropriate, to tailor the job for individual needs. For example, you require a 7:30 start time but you've found an ideal candidate who can't start till 7:45 — a compromise you may choose to make.

- Your Job Description can easily become your Work Agreement once you've selected a candidate. A written agreement may sound formal and impersonal — especially at the start when things are looking great — but this agreement is very important to you as an employer (more on that topic in the "Manage With Care" section).

- You can use your Job Description to guide you and your nanny through the first few weeks on the job, usually an evaluation period. You can go through the list of tasks on a daily or weekly basis to judge how things are going and make minor adjustments along the way.

The next pages contain a sample Job Description that is fairly detailed. Following the Description, you will find a Sample Cover Letter in the event you wish to send the Job Description out to candidates in advance of their personal interview. Remember, the point is not to write a Pulitzer Prize winning novel! Rather, your objective is to be clear and complete about your expectations.

Dear Prospective Nanny:

Thank you for your interest in our position for a live-out nanny!

Getting the right person for this job is currently our number one family priority. To help you better understand our expectations, we have compiled the enclosed Job Description. Please take your time reviewing this information and feel free to note any questions or concerns you may have. We realize that it's very detailed - but this gives both you and us the chance to thoroughly cover every aspect of the position to make sure we each make the right decision.

Once again, we appreciate your time and we are looking forward to learning more about you in our upcoming interview.

Sincerely,

Dave and Diane Keefe

JOB DESCRIPTION

JOB DESCRIPTION: LIVE-OUT NANNY
General Requirements

Your primary responsibility is to be the full time caretaker for Jennifer, our two-year-old daughter. You will come to our home, from 7:45 am to 5:45 pm, on Monday through Friday (evenings and weekends are not required). We have deliberately chosen an in-home arrangement because we believe it offers the best environment for our child.

You will play a vital role in our family which requires these key qualifications:

- You must *enjoy children*! While there are certain aspects of taking care of children which are not fun, we want someone who truly takes an interest in Jennifer and wants the best for her as we do.

- You must be *enthusiastic, conscientious, and caring.*

- You must take a *personal interest and pride* in your contribution to our family. We want someone who will get to know Jennifer as an individual — understand her nature, personality, habits, likes and dislikes.

- You must be able to *communicate openly and honestly*. We want you to be comfortable discussing issues with us — telling us how things go between you and Jennifer; and taking our input and direction. We hope you are willing to let us get to know you too.

- We require someone who will *take initiative* and support our family environment. If you think Jennifer would love to go to a special show; or if she needs some special attention from 'mom'; or if she's suddenly outgrown all her clothes — say so!

The following also applies:

- NON-SMOKERS only please!

- You must be prompt and dependable.

- On occasion, you may be asked to come in earlier or stay later. We always appreciate any flexibility you can offer but also respect your personal schedule.

Specific Duties & Responsibilities

Child Care:

Supervising at ALL TIMES

Planning Activities

Food Preparation

Dressing/Bathing

Providing Transportation

Handling Medical Needs

Imparting Discipline

Teaching Manners

JOB DESCRIPTION

Child-Related Housekeeping Duties:

Transportation

Straightening-up

Laundry

Cleaning

Shopping/Errands

Cooking

Considerations For The Nanny:

Personal Activities

Personal Appointments

Personal Meals

Following you will find a detailed explanation of each of these duties and responsibilities. During your interview, we will use this information to further review the position, your qualifications, and any input or concerns you may have.

JOB DESCRIPTION

Responsibilities   Notes

Direct Supervision:

Supervise and interact with Jennifer on a full time basis. This includes responsibilities for health and well being as well as play and educational activities.

We'll expect a written log of her activities (playing, eating, sleeping) during the day.

Planning Activities:

Plan and participate in activities to stimulate emotional, mental, and physical growth for Jennifer. These activities should occur both in and outside the home.

Examples:

- reading at home
- regular library visits
- museum, zoo visits

Television viewing is not an acceptable activity.

Food Preparation:

Plan and provide daily meals (breakfast, lunch, and snack) with appropriate nutrition. All food will be provided and

JOB DESCRIPTION

Responsibilities   **Notes**

any special requests or preferences will
be discussed with you regularly. You
are expected to take the time to
encourage healthy nutritional habits and
manners with Jennifer.

Dressing/Bathing:

Perform daily dressing routine including
washing up, brushing teeth and hair.
Baths typically won't be necessary
however you must make cleanliness a
priority!

Handling Medical Needs:

You will administer medication to
Jennifer (over the counter or
prescription) ONLY if we have provided
written instructions to do so.

In the event of a medical emergency
you are to contact us immediately. If
necessary, call for assistance first
(doctor, ambulance), and then notify us.

Discipline:

Our goal is for you to be consistent with
our parenting style in all areas, but
discipline is especially important. This
is a topic which we will discuss very

Responsibilities

Notes

frequently to understand where and how we can best focus on Jennifer's behavior. You will be expected to enforce rules for her safety, play activities, manners, eating and sleeping habits, etc. You will also be expected to use good judgment at all times, and to review any concerns or questions with us promptly. This will help you to understand our preference, but it will also help us understand what Jennifer needs.

PHYSICAL DISCIPLINE OF ANY KIND IS FORBIDDEN.

You will discipline first by *REDIRECTING* Jennifer's attention or energy away from the inappropriate behavior. A simple but firm explanation/discussion (depending on the offense) should reinforce what behavior is and isn't acceptable.

If Redirection isn't effective, then you will use a *TIMEOUT* to get her into a neutral space and away from the situation for an appropriate period of time.

Responsibilities   **Notes**

Manners:

Teaching and reinforcing good manners
can be a part of discipline but is also an
important part of Jennifer's education.
You will be expected to participate in
helping her to understand courtesy,
politeness, and how to interact with
others.

Transportation:

Creating a healthy and positive
environment in our home is very
important. However, we also want
Jennifer to have opportunities for fun
and learning outside of the home on a
regular basis. Planning activities
outside the home should be an area of
interest for you.   Therefore, you must
have a safe and reliable means of
transportation available at all times.
Also, use of a car seat (we will provide)
with Jennifer in your car is required at all
times.

Housekeeping:

Our house and family is your workplace
so we'll ask that you participate in
'upkeep' activities, especially those
directly related to Jennifer. You are not

JOB DESCRIPTION

Responsibilities   **Notes**

a housekeeper - we have a regular one. However, young children create havoc quite easily and you should be willing to pick up and maintain a reasonable degree of neatness and appearance. By helping out in these areas, you'll increase the time we have to spend with our child.

Straightening Up:

You are expected to 'straighten up' rooms, toys, and clothes related to Jennifer's and your own activities on a daily basis.

Laundry:

You will handle Jennifer's regular laundry twice a week. This includes washing, drying, folding, and putting away her clothes. Also, if something gets soiled unexpectedly (spot on the carpet, a spill on her or the furniture, etc.), you should get it cleaned and replaced promptly.

Cleaning:

While you are not responsible for the housekeeping, we ask that you keep the kitchen, play areas (in and out), and

Responsibilities   ***Notes***

Jennifer's room in good shape. In general, any mess created during the day should be picked up promptly.

Shopping/Errands:

You may be asked to assist in minor shopping or errands during the week.

Personal Activities:

Your responsibilities are full time, five days a week, and you are expected to be 'working' 100% of the time. However, activities for yourself can be a part of your day as long as you are meeting all your job duties and there isn't any inconvenience or adverse effect on Jennifer.

If there is anything in our home you are not permitted to use, we will bring it to your attention. If you have something you wish to bring to or leave at our home we will try to accommodate it. In all cases, we'll want to discuss your activities *in advance* to be sure they are acceptable.

JOB DESCRIPTION

Responsibilities   *Notes*

Personal Appointments:

You may not have personal visitors at our home nor go to personal appointments with Jennifer. If you have personal appointments which cannot be scheduled after work, please give us as much advance notice as possible and we will work our schedules to help you out!

Personal Meals/Other:

We expect you to provide for your own meals, however you are welcome to general food items in the house. The best rule of thumb is: if there is anything you eat in quantity or regularly - bring it. For example, if you drink two cans of soda a week, you may help yourself to the family stock. If you drink a six-pack a day then you should plan to provide your own.

THE COST OF IN-HOME CARE

There are many dimensions associated with the true cost of your child 's care:

- Peace Of Mind
- Wages
- Taxes
- Social Security
- Medicare
- Insurance
- Benefits

With the exception of your peace of mind, these are specific, real costs which you must evaluate from a budgetary standpoint. Make every effort to clearly identify the limits and possible compromises you are willing to make to meet your child care goals within your budget.

This section discusses each of these cost dimensions in greater detail.

Peace Of Mind

A live-out nanny is relatively more expensive than other options if you consider the cost only in terms of the dollars you spend each month.   However, there are some benefits of an in-home arrangement that don't translate directly into dollar costs, but do have a big impact on your peace of mind. Consider these less tangible costs when comparing a nanny to other forms of care:

- Many studies show that children who remain at home are healthier than those in other child care environments. This is particularly the case for young children — newborn to toddler age. There is a dollar cost (more trips to the doctor, medicine, time off work) as well as an emotional cost associated with having a sick child.

- Children and parents usually suffer from separation anxiety regardless of the child care arrangements. However, this emotional stress is often increased when combined with difficult adjustments to teachers, other children, and a community environment.

- In many day care settings, there is high staff turn-over making it difficult for your child to bond adequately with his caretaker. It also means that your child's unique needs or interests are less likely to be understood and responded to.

- Day care centers have large groups of children together in a single room. Even a relatively small group can cause a child to feel anxious and lost in the crowd due to the noise alone.

- With other day care arrangements, you often have to work within a schedule which isn't accommodating to you or your child. Dragging your child out of bed, forcing breakfast down, and putting him into the car often isn't an ideal way to start either his or your day. It can be a daily hassle to coordinate work or travel schedules to deposit or collect your child within the stipulated times. All of this contributes to unneeded anxiety and aggravation for everyone.

Each child care option offers a different combination of both tangible and intangible costs and benefits. Once again, these can only be evaluated according to your own family priorities. Parents who have selected a live-out nanny are likely to pay more dollars but will gain some unique benefits in return. You will be more comfortable with your decision on how much to pay your nanny if you keep these unique benefits in mind.

How Much Should I Pay?

The wage rate for a live-out nanny will vary depending on several factors. Her experience and educational qualifications are the most important factors you should consider. Be prepared to pay more for someone with a Childhood Education Degree and 10 years' experience as a nanny, than for someone who is highly recommended, but has no formal training and only a few years on the job.

Other factors which influence pay relate to your job description. You will pay more or less depending on how attractive or unattractive your arrangement is:

- does your location necessitate a lengthy commute?

- how many children is she responsible for and what are their ages?

- do you require light, moderate, or heavy non-child related duties (housework, running errands, and so on)?

- how many hours a week will she be expected to be at work? does this include weeknights or weekends?

- what kind of benefits are you offering in addition to wages?

In most geographies, hourly wages range from $5.00 to $7.00 an hour for an average 50-hour week (7:30 a.m. to 5:30 p.m., Monday through Friday). Salaries for the same work schedule will range from $900.00 to $1,600.00 a month. These estimates assume there's nothing extreme about your requirements, and should be used as a guideline only.

There are a few things you can do to more accurately define the 'going' rate. Call several nanny advertisements in the classifieds and ask the employers what they are paying. Talk with local nanny placement agencies about the pay range for their candidates. Ask friends and colleagues who have (or had) nannies. Finally, ask references for their input on wages and benefits.

Salary Versus Hourly Wages

You can pay your nanny either a fixed salary or hourly wages (for actual number of hours worked). In addition to a possible cost difference, here are some other considerations to help you decide:

- By paying hourly, you pay only for what you use. You may choose to include paid time off for holidays or vacations as a benefit.

- You will have to maintain a record of hours worked and calculate wages each pay period (whether weekly, bimonthly, or monthly) if you pay hourly wages. This can be time consuming on your part.

- Usually, anything over ten hours on a single day is considered overtime and paid for at a higher rate than the normal wage. Take this into account when comparing costs.

- Nannies who rely on their wages as a primary source of income tend to prefer a salary arrangement over hourly. This is especially true if your schedule varies significantly each week, resulting in an unpredictable paycheck for her.

- Sometimes a salary arrangement will promote a tendency for tardiness or increased personal time off for your nanny, as she is paid regardless of actual time on the job. On the other hand, an hourly arrangement can foster a different problem. Your nanny may consistently arrive earlier and stay longer than necessary, or she may resent the occasional afternoon you come home early because it cuts into her paycheck.

As with any aspect of hiring a nanny, make your wage decision in accordance with your family's priorities. Then be sure to communicate your expectations around her pay *very clearly* to your nanny during the interview process and then again when she starts to work for you.

✳ Benefits

Here's a list of possible benefits you might consider offering your nanny. Some of these don't require a direct outlay of cash on your part, but do enhance your offer. You may include benefits in your initial offer or introduce them to reward a job well done over time.

- *Vacation*

  You can offer a certain number of paid vacation days in a given period. For example, you may offer one day a month paid time off (every second Thursday perhaps). Another option is to give five days a year paid vacation to be taken at her discretion. You should also determine how much advance notification you require prior to her vacation.

  If you have elected to pay her on a salary, you should agree and document how vacation time (both yours and hers) will be handled. For example, if you plan on taking three weeks off for the Christmas holidays, do you intend to pay her full salary during that time?

  If you are paying an hourly wage, be sure to define the number of hours that constitute a 'day'. For example, if her normal work schedule is 7:30 am to 5:30 p.m., then consider a day of paid time off as 10 hours. This applies to personal time and holidays as well.

✳ • *Personal Time Off*

Personal time off covers any time that isn't considered pre-planned vacation. This would include doctor appointments, sick days, an illness or death in her family, and other personal activities which conflict with her work schedule. Whether you are paying a salary or hourly wage, be sure to define how you expect her to handle personal time off, and how you will pay (or not pay) accordingly.

✳ • *Holidays*

There are two issues on this topic. First, which ones will she have off? You should identify those holidays when you will not require her services. Also, what days are you including? Is Christmas just the 25th, or the 24th too?

The second issue is which holidays, if any, do you consider as paid holidays? This isn't an issue if you are paying a salary. However, if you are paying hourly wages, you have the option of including some holidays as paid time off.

• *Club Membership*

If you have a family health club membership, you may be able to include your nanny at no charge. Or, you may be willing to pay an incremental fee to include her so that she and your child can participate in club activities.

✳ • *Gas or Mileage Reimbursement*

If you expect your nanny to do a lot of traveling on your child's behalf or on errands, you might want to provide reimbursement.

- *Entertainment Expenses*

Determine how you want to handle the cost of activities for her and your child.   If you are encouraging outside activities you should plan on paying for her participation. If it's the zoo followed by lunch at McDonald's — pick up the cost for admission and two Happy Meals!

You may want to set a dollar limit that she can spend without prior approval and keep a 'petty cash fund' available.   Alternatively, you may choose to review proposed expenditures on a weekly basis.

- *Health Insurance*

Although this can be an expensive benefit, it is very vaulable to most employees. If you offer health insurance coverage to you nanny, you may be able to reduce other benefits or even her salary Check into your employer's group plan to determine if you can include your nanny as a family member. You can also contact local agencies to determine if they use a group plan that is available to individuals.

Becoming An Employer

If you hire a nanny, you *must* become an Employer as defined by the state and federal governments. As an Employer you will file tax forms, and pay taxes (if you are withholding), Social Security, Medicare, and unemployment insurance.

There are Federal Internal Revenue Service guidelines and regulations for the tax liabilities associated with Employers of domestic services. *It is highly recommended that you review the current IRS guidelines and regulations to determine your obligations.*   To obtain detailed information, call the IRS

Information Line for your region or state or contact the IRS General Information hotline at (800) 829-1040. You can also have the following publications and forms mailed to you from the Federal IRS Warehouse by calling (800) 829-FORM:

- Publication 115 (Circular E) Employer's Tax Guide
- Publication 926 Employment Taxes for Household Employers

Most state tax agencies publish 'Getting Started As An Employer' Guides which are invaluable to beginners. They provide step by step instructions on meeting your obligations. You can also contact state and federal employer help lines as they generally are very informative and polite. Finally, don't forget your accountant — he or she can be a fountain of information.

The specific costs associated with being an employer fall into these categories: Social Security, Medicare, State and Federal Unemployment Taxes, and Workman's Compensation Insurance. As you evaluate the costs, don't forget the time required for you to maintain records and file quarterly and annual forms in accordance with IRS and state regulations.

At first glance, this looks about as much fun as filling out your annual tax return — and even more confusing! Without a doubt, it takes some time to get used to the forms, regulations, and mumbo jumbo. There are two secrets to success here: get organized from the start, and don't be shy about asking for help.

Here is a summary list to help you get familiar with the required activities you must perform as an employer. Following is an explanation for each item.

What To Do:	*When To Do It:*
Get a Federal Employer's Identification Number (Form SS-4 or Form 942)	When you decide to hire a nanny
Get a State Employer's Identification Number	When you decide to hire a nanny
Complete the Immigration and Naturalization Service's I9 Form	Within 3 days of nanny's hire date
Complete From W-4, Employee's Withholding Allowance Certificate	By hire date
Purchase Workman's Compenstation Insurance	By hire date
Set up payroll records	By hire date
Calculate Social Security and Medicare withholding from each paycheck	Performed each pay period
Calculate State and Federal tax withholding (optional)	Performed each pay period
File Form 942 to pay Federal taxes withheld	Quarterly
File State Forms to pay state taxes withheld and any unemployment taxes due	Quarterly
File Federal Unemployment Tax Return - Form 940 or 940-EZ	Annually
Complete W-2 Wage and Tax Statement and W-3 Transmittal Form	Annually

1. *Get a Federal Employer's Identification Number (FEIN)*: This is assigned by the IRS. The FEIN is used to establish your federal income tax withholding, Social Security and Medicare withholding, and federal unemployement account with the IRS.   It can be obtained in one of two ways:

   - Complete Federal Form SS-4 and forward to the IRS. You will receive your FEIN in approximately four weeks.

   - Complete your first Quarterly Employment Tax Form 942 as required and write "NONE" in the FEIN space. The IRS will automatically assign a number and send you a tax form each quarter with your name, address, and FEIN preprinted on the lable.

2. *Get a State Identification Number* : Most states require an employer identification number to open accounts for taxes and unemployment payments. Contact your state's Department of Revenue for instructions on obtaining an employer's identification number.

3. *Complete the Immigration and Naturalization Service's I9 Form*: This must be completed within three working days after employment begins. It's purpose is to ensure that employer's do not hire illegal aliens. As such, it requires the employee to provide specific documents to the employer to verify residency and to confirm they are eligible for employment in the United States. Get this signed and save it in your nanny's file for at least three years after the date of hiring or one year after she is terminated, whichever is later. Further information, and a copy of the I9 form can be obtained by calling the INS at (800) 755-0777.

4. *Complete Form W-4, Employee's Withholding Allowance Certificate*: This must be filled out and signed by your nanny to indicate her marital status and the number of exemptions she will claim for tax withholding purposes. You are not required to withhold Federal taxes unless both of you want it done, however she still must complete and sign the W-4. In most states, if you are not withholding Federal taxes, you are not required to withhold state taxes. If you do not withhold tax, your nanny is still responsible for paying any taxes due with her annual income tax return.

5. *Set up Workman's Compenstation Insurance Coverage:* This insurance covers your nanny should she become injured while on the job. As an employer you are responsible for providing a policy with appropriate coverage. Many states have a Workman's Compensation Authority which offers a policy for a household employees. These can run approximately $500 per year. Private insurance companies are usually less (anywhere from $300 to $400).

6. *Set up your Payroll Records*: Every time you pay your nanny, you must keep a record of her gross earnings and the amount of social security, medicare, and withholding taxes collected.   Set up a register which makes it convenient for you to write everything down each time you write her check. The IRS requires that you keep all records of employment taxes for at least 4 years.

7. *Calculate Social Security and Medicare Withholding:* You will need to figure out how much to withhold from each paycheck for Social Security and Medicare. Once you have computed her wages (based either on her salary or hours worked), deduct the following:

- 6.2% of gross wages for Social Security

- 1.45% of gross wages for Medicare

8. *Calculate Federal and State Withholding:* If you are withholding taxes, you will also need to figure the correct amount for each paycheck. Use the federal withholding tax tables (included in Circular E, Employer's Tax Guide) and the appropriate state tax table to determine the tax amount based on her marital status and exemptions claimed on the W-4.

9. *File Federal Form 942 and the necessary State Forms each Quarter:* As an employer, you must match the employee's contribution for Social Security and Medicare. You will make a payment of 15.3% of total wages (half having been withheld from the employee, and the other half being your portion) on a quarterly basis by completing Form 942. If you have withheld taxes, you will use Form 942 to pay them to the IRS each quarter as well.

10. *File State Unemployment Taxes each Quarter:* Most states require unemployment taxes on a quarterly basis. This information will be included in your state's getting started business kit. The tax is typically less than 5 percent of wages.

11. *File Federal Unemployment Tax Return (Form 940 or 940 EZ)*: This is filed annually. The rate is 6.2% of wages paid during the year. Generally, you can take a credit against your FUTA for amounts you paid into your state unemployment fund. This can result in a FUTA rate as low as .8 percent.

12. *Complete the W-2 Wage and Tax Statement Form at year end*: This summarizes the wages, Social Security, Medicare, and income taxes withheld (if any) for the year. Your nanny will include the W-2 in her personal tax returns.

13. *File W-3 Transmittal of Income and Tax Statements at year end*: The W-3 is completed and sent, along with a copy of the W-2, to the Social Security Administration. You may also be required to complete a similar form for your state.

Getting set up as an Employer will require some time on your part so you may want to plan ahead before you start interviewing. If you do hire a nanny before all your paperwork is complete, be sure to keep accurate and detailed records of her wages.

Once again, this information has been provided to familiarize you with the costs and responsibilities in becoming an Employer. Utilize the Federal IRS and State information to ensure your are fully compliant with all regulations.

FINDING THE RIGHT NANNY

After much preparation, you are confident in your decision for a live-out nanny, and feel comfortable in your expectations about the job. Now you're ready to embark on the search for the perfect nanny!

There are several ways you can go about your search, ranging in cost from minimal to fairly expensive. One option is to use an agency or service specializing in helping parents find child care providers. The following section is included to help you understand the costs and benefits of using such an agency. Because these costs can be significant, many parents prefer to conduct a search on their own. Therefore, the remaining sections are dedicated to information and suggestions for finding the right nanny by yourself.

Using An Agency

An agency typically provides some combination of the following services:

- Maintain an active database of available candidates with a wide range of qualifications

- Perform background checks on the candidates which can include driving record, criminal or legal records, education, and references

- Pre-screen candidates based on your job requirements

- Set up interviews and assist in your evaluation

- Assist in employment arrangements and contracts

These services can reduce the time and effort you must invest to find qualified candidates and set up interviews. The cost varies depending on the service, but a typical range would be from $ 150 (a reference fee for connecting parents and nannies) to $1500 or more (a full service fee for placement or contracting of professional nannies).

Keep these points in mind if you are considering an agency:

- Using an agency won't necessarily cut down on the time frame it takes you to find a nanny. The time-consuming part of your search — interviewing — is the same whether an agency finds good candidates or you do so yourself.

- An agency gets candidates the same way you would — by advertising and through references — so don't assume they will automatically provide a higher quality candidate. The only exception will be agencies associated with a nanny school or training program where graduates work exclusively through that agency. It is a benefit to you if the agency performs some of the background checks. However, you will still want to personally confirm the integrity and quality of any candidate you wish to hire.

- Most nannies looking for work will register with multiple agencies but also keep an eye on the classifieds for possible openings. Therefore, you may find the same candidate through your own advertising at the much lower cost of an ad versus the agency fee. National agencies do offer a broader database if they include candidates looking to move into your geography from elsewhere. Au pairs from other countries use both agencies and informal networks when looking for work in the United States.

- Be sure you understand all the costs and obligations associated with any agency you choose to work with. For example, what happens if you pay a placement fee and your nanny quits after three weeks? Or, are you restricted in any way in the nature or cost of your employment contract with the nanny because of the agency? Get all of the facts up front and if possible, ask to talk to other parents who have used the agency.

For the most part, there is nothing an agency can do that you can't do for yourself — it's just a matter of time and money.

Timing

"When should I start looking and how long will it take to find a nanny?" This is a very common question with a simple, but not very helpful answer: *"It depends."*

You'll be off to a good start if you have accomplished the tasks outlined in the "Defining the Job" section of this Guide. You can also put some advance thought and research into what kind of employment arrangement you want (refer to "The Cost of In-home Care") although many of those decisions may depend on your candidate.

The time it takes to start lining up interviews depends on your advertising activities. An ad in Sunday's paper might bring an avalanche of calls on Monday morning, while a poster at Church might generate some interest the following weekend. In-home child care is a popular option for both parents and child care providers, so most likely you will experience a plentiful response.

The biggest factor in timing will be the number of candidates you must interview to find the right one which is difficult to predict. A general rule of thumb is to start interviewing four to eight weeks before you need a nanny. If you plan much farther ahead, you'll be limiting your options to those candidates who know they will be available several months from now. If you wait too long, you maybe tempted to compromise on quality to meet your time frame.

Don't panic if you're at one extreme or the other — the nature of the job works in your favor. Both you and the candidates want a good 'chemistry' together. When there's a mutual fit, you'll share a natural enthusiasm to resolve any immediate scheduling conflicts.

Advertising And Networking

You know the perfect nanny is out there — it's just a matter of tracking her down. So advertise where she is likely to be or look, and network with people who are likely to know her.

- The classified section of your local newspapers include "Domestic Services" or "Child Care Employment" advertisements. Write a creative ad which summarizes your requirements and be sure to run it in the weekend editions (when the greatest number of people use the classifieds).

- Local day care centers often have information about nannies looking for work. Or you may find day care teachers looking to change to a private arrangement.

- Check out community and specialty publications which also have classifieds. Don't forget college, schools, and church newsletters. Many community colleges have two-year programs in early child care.

- In addition to placing your own add, review the "Situations Wanted" advertisements. Some nannies will advertise their services or availability in this manner.

- Post flyers on bulletin boards at your church, club, or other social organizations where you participate. Be careful to advertise within organizations which reflect your values and lifestyle.

- Many pediatricians have a bulletin board or newsletter with information about child care. Any professional practice or business serving parents or children can offer an opportunity to advertise and network.

- Let family and friends know you are looking, especially those who have nannies already. Many times an employed nanny is an excellent source of recently or about-to-be unemployed nannies.

- If you are interested in a mature nanny, look into Senior Citizens centers and organizations.

- Don't overlook your obstetrician or hospital, especially if you are a new parent. Many maternity programs include information and contacts for local child care. Some will even pay the registration fee or entire cost of an agency as a benefit to mothers who select their maternity program.

Here are two sample ads which can be used in the classifieds section of a newspaper:

Nanny Needed: Live out, full time. Must be reliable, experienced, and loving to care for 2 yr. old. Excel. pay for qualified candidates. Ref's req'd. Call 555-1234

West Hills Area: Full time, live out nanny to care for 6 mo. old and 3 yr. old. Non-smoker, high energy, and experience a must. Qual. candidates with ref's only please. 555-1234

If you advertise on a bulletin board, you can include more information about the position. Remember to make it easy for interested parties to get back with you. Use tear-off tabs or attach a stack of sticky notes with your phone number on the flyer.

NANNY NEEDED

We are looking for a nanny to care for our 6-month-old son and 3-year-old daughter. This is a full time, live-out position. We require someone with experience as a nanny to provide a loving and stimulating environment for our children in our home. You must be reliable, neat, and a non-smoker. If you meet these qualifications and have outstanding references please give us a call at 555-1234!

Interviewing — Helpful Hints

For many parents, this step in finding a nanny is the most difficult. Interviewing is demanding and time-consuming. It can be awkward and frustrating, but also interesting and exciting. Here's some simple advice to make it a positive experience:

- *Be prepared.*

There is no better way to be comfortable and productive during interviews than being fully prepared. Your confidence will reassure the candidate and facilitate a sincere, open dialog. You'll demonstrate the commitment and involvement you bring to your child's care, thereby setting the stage for what you expect from your nanny. The time you invest to become prepared will be more than returned in the quantity and quality of information you gain from interviews.

- *Be patient.*

Set aside your time and full attention for your interviewing activities. If you are anxious or distracted, you may miss a subtle, but critical clue about the potential of a candidate. While it's important to listen to your instinct, recognize that it takes time for your instinct to 'tune in' and give you a good reading.

- *Be yourself.*

There will be many facets to your relationship with your nanny. Sometimes you will have to sort through inherent conflicts which exist in your role as parent, employer and family to this person. By just being yourself during the interview process, you'll create an honest and realistic foundation upon which to build an effective working relationship over time.

This advice applies to the whole family, especially your child. If your two-year-old tends to be on the rambunctious side, don't present him as a quiet, reserved child. You'll want a nanny with the energy and good humor to keep up with him — not one who prefers a quiet, reserved child!

Reach Out And Touch Someone

The process of interviewing a potential candidate starts with your first interaction, usually a phone conversation in response to an ad or reference. Your objective for this step is to determine if you want to pursue her further with a personal interview.

Begin the conversation by introducing yourself and briefly stating your requirements. It's important to outline your job requirements right away to avoid wasting your precious time on people who are merely looking for work. It will become readily apparent if a candidate is a casual baby-sitter or bored grandmother; only the serious, dedicated nannies will calmly accept your description.

Once the candidate has passed this first qualification, explain what your objective is for this conversation. For example:

"Mary, thank you for calling in response to our ad! My name is Diane Keefe. My husband David and I are looking for a full time live-out nanny for our two-year-old son Matthew. We expect someone who is committed to all aspects of Matthew's care - including his health, education, and entertainment. Your typical day will start at 7:30 and end at 5:30 We do require some light housework. Is this the kind of position you are interested in?"

(yes.)

"Great. What I'd like to do is take a few minutes to talk about your qualifications. Is now a good time or would you prefer to schedule a phone conversation later today?"

From here on out, you'll want to gather data about her credentials and formulate a first impression to get a sense for her compatibility with your requirements. Here is a list of questions and information you can use during a telephone interview. The right column is intentionally left blank to provide room for your notes and comments. Write things down during the interview or immediately after. Don't count on remembering either data or your impressions for a candidate — it's far too easy to get mixed up after three or four interviews!!

PHONE INTERVIEW

Applicant Information

Name: _____	Phone: _____
Address: _____	City: _____
State: _____	Zip: _____
Referred By: _____	Date: _____

General	*Notes*
• Do you smoke?	
• Do you have a valid driver's license? Do you have a reliable car? Is it insured?	
• Are you allergic to pets or unwilling to be around them?	

PHONE INTERVIEW

• What area of town do you live in? (Will her commute be unreasonable?)	
• Other	

Experience   **Notes**

• What kind of child care experience do you have?	
• What age children have you worked with?	
• Do you have any formal training or education for child care?	

• Do you have CPR training or any first aid training? Do you have a certificate?	
• Do you have your own children? What are their ages?	
• Tell me about your most recent position.	
• Why did you leave your last position?	
• What other jobs have you held?	

PHONE INTERVIEW

Requirements	Notes
• We are interested in a long term arrangement. What kind of time frame are you interested in? What are your future plans?	
• Your schedule would be from _____ to _____. (Note any possible exceptions or fluctuations.) Do you see any problem meeting this schedule?	
• What is your availability to start a full time position?	
• What are your salary requirements? (If appropriate, give a range in hourly or salary wages.)	
• Other	

PHONE INTERVIEW

At this point you should decide if she:

Is not good fit ....

"I really appreciate your taking the time to chat with me today. You have very good qualifications, however, I don't feel that we can offer you the type of position you require. Thank you again and good luck."

Looks promising ....

"Based on our conversation so far, I feel you have many of the qualifications we are looking for. We may be interested in setting up a personal interview. However, before we do, I'd like to ask a few more questions about yourself as well as get some reference information."

Personal	*Notes*

• What do you consider to be your strengths as a nanny? Look for these words in her description or prompt her if she needs it:
 	
  - reliable
  - creative
  - loves children
  - caring
  - energetic	

PHONE INTERVIEW

- What do you like most
  about being a nanny?

- What do you like least
  about being a nanny?

General Comments & Follow Up Notes

References

Name: _____   Phone: _____

Name: _____   Phone: _____

Name: _____   Phone: _____

PHONE INTERVIEW

When It's Not A Fit

If at any point you or the candidate determine that further discussion is inappropriate, be prepared to politely end the conversation:

> *"Terry, I realize that not everyone is a dog lover and I appreciate your honesty. However, Dottie is an important part of our family and we feel it's best to hire someone who shares our affection for dogs. Thank you for your time and good luck."*

or ...

> *"Margaret, you certainly seem to have excellent qualifications, but I'm afraid our budget won't accommodate your salary requirements. I do appreciate your time today and wish you luck finding a position."*

When It Might Be A Fit

So far, everything sounds good, and you think you want a personal interview, but you're not totally convinced. Don't hesitate to probe her more directly in the area where you have a concern or sense she is unsure:

> *"Mary, we had planned on paying on an hourly basis, but it sounds like you were more interested in a salary. Is that a firm requirement or would you consider discussing it further?"*

or ...

*"I'm concerned about the fact that you live
almost 30 minutes away. How do you feel
about that kind of commute?"*

or ...

*"You have a lot of experience with children,
but you've only worked with at most two at
one time. Let's talk about how you would
handle three on a full time basis."*

If you are still unsure about a possible fit, confirm your interest
and indicate that you will get back to her in the event you desire
additional discussions. Consider asking her for a reference. Often,
a previous employer can help clarify your interest one way or the
other. (More on references to come.)

Finally, be sure to ask her about her time frame and find out if she
is currently anticipating offers. In return, tell her what your time
frame is.

It's A Fit!

You like what you've heard and you want to get to know this
person better. *Now* is the time to get references! It's always best
to check references before a personal interview, because:

- some people are very good at interviewing, but fall
short of expectations on the job;

- you can prepare a more thorough interview by
including information you gather from the reference;

- you may uncover something which completely changes
your mind about the candidate.

References

References are a must when you are looking for a nanny. Your conversations with a reference can often be very enlightening and enjoyable. If they recently employed a nanny, they share your concerns for quality care, and as a result, are eager to help out a fellow parent in need.

You should call as many references as possible, especially if you are serious about a candidate. If she doesn't supply a previous employer as a reference, proceed with caution and find out why that is the case. Some situations do end on a bad note, but this does not automatically reflect negatively on her. Be on guard for signs of a pattern of performance or attitude problems which account for poor relations with previous employers.

Here's a list of questions to help in your conversation with references.

REFERENCE INTERVIEW

Applicant Name: _____

Reference Name: _____

General	Notes
• How did you hear about her?	
• How long did you employ her?	
• How many children did she care for?	
• What were her hours?	
• What kind of wage arrangement did you have (hourly or salary?)	

REFERENCE INTERVIEW

• What caused you to let her go?	
• Other	

Experience   **Notes**

• How would you rate your experience with her and why? (Fair, Good, Excellent)	
• What did your children like about her? What did they dislike?	

• Is she safety conscious? Did you ever have any occasion to worry about the health or safety of your child while in her care?	
• How would you describe her family situation? Was it ever disruptive to her work?	
• How would you describe her attitude about her work? Is she: - energetic - conscientious - happy - self-motivated - flexible	

REFERENCE INTERVIEW

• Did she take direction and input from you well?	
• Did she give you feedback on your child's activities and growth?	
• How would you describe her work habits? Is she: - neat - considerate - punctual - reliable	
• How would you expect her to handle an emergency or unusual situation?	

REFERENCE INTERVIEW

• Do you have any reservations about her ability as a child care provider?	
• Would you hire her again?	

General Comments & Follow Up Notes

REFERENCE INTERVIEW

Don't hesitate to have a follow up conversation with a reference once you've had a personal interview with your candidate. You may uncover an area where you can benefit from their insight. For example:

> *"While Mary and I were talking, she mentioned an incident with your son that sounded pretty scary. I understand he hit his head at the play ground and she had to call the ambulance and go with him to the hospital. How do you feel she handled the situation? Did you have any concerns about negligence on her part?"*

or ...

> *"We like the fact that Jan likes to plan activities for the kids. But we are concerned about having her out of the house a lot. Do you feel confident in her driving habits? Does she use good judgment when it comes to safety or having the kids around strangers?"*

Up Close And Personal

Set up the personal interview at a mutually convenient time, preferably in your own home. As in your previous conversations, briefly explain what you expect to accomplish and how much time the candidate should set aside. Thirty minutes is a fair estimate, but you could go longer if there is mutual interest.

If time permits, send her a copy of your Job Description prior to the personal interview. This will enable her to review it ahead of time and come prepared with questions. It is possible that she'll decide the job is not for her after all and cancel the interview. Refer to the Cover Letter provided at the end of the Job Description.

Once she has agreed to the interview, she may ask you if you are prepared to make an offer if all goes well with the interview. Be both honest and flexible. If you have another candidate you are seriously considering, let her know. If she is considering another position and needs to know your decision immediately, you may have to be prepared to act quickly. Be sure to take time as a family to discuss your impressions after the interview. If necessary, politely ask her to step out of the room and talk it out together. She may use this time to fill out an Employment Application (refer to the next section).

Here are a few final pointers to help you prepare for your interviews:

- Organize your information ahead of time. Have a copy of your Job Description. Include your notes from your phone interviews with her and her references. Write down any questions you have based on your initial conversation or which came up during your reference discussions.

- The Job Description is the easiest guide for your interview questions. However, you may wish to add some situational questions such as "what would you do if ...?" These questions help you to further assess her experience level and to gain insight into her child care philosophy. Include age specific situations which are relevant to your child's age.

- Set up the interview so that both parents can participate. Sometimes it is easier to have one parent direct the questions while the other takes notes. You should agree ahead of time on a polite 'termination' tactic in the event one of you is convinced there isn't a good fit.

- Consider introducing your child after you've had a few minutes alone with the candidate to chat — he can pose a distraction for you while you're trying to get oriented and comfortable together. Depending on his age, you may want to suggest a few questions he can ask her directly. This gives him the opportunity to be involved, and you'll be able to observe her style of interaction with children. Someone who works well with children will squat down to meet the child at his eye level. Be on the look out for this kind of behavior and watch your child's reaction. A child will make an instinctive, and usually very accurate, assessment of a candidate based on this initial exchange.

- Listen, listen, listen! Resist the temptation to do most of the talking. If you encourage her to ask questions, her major areas of concern or interest will become obvious as your conversation progresses. Does she ask about the kids? the parents? the salary and benefits package? In addition to understanding her priorities, the personal interview is your best opportunity to detemine if your mutual ability to communicate will be comfortable and effective.

Making A Selection

An Employment Application provides yet another source of information about the candidate. You can use it at any time during your selection process, however you will most likely have only those candidates which are under serious consideration fill it out.

Following, you will find a sample Application which includes some important information you may not have asked for during your interviews. As you review the application, remember these considerations:

- Information about a candidate's driving record, educational background and personal situation is very useful in assessing her integrity. If she refuses to provide such information, this may be an indication of something in her past which is inconsistent with the level of integrity or capability you want in a nanny.

- A social security number must be provided if you, as an employer, are to meet your obligations for State and Federal tax, social security, Medicare, and unemployment insurance. You will also use this to take advantage of IRS tax credits for child care. You can use a social security number to run a credit check on a candidate. However you must obtain her permission *in writing* to perform such a check.

- If she lists special child care education, follow up with the indicated institution to confirm her claim.

- Employment discrimination is a topic you should be familiar with. The Federal Government has strict Equal Employment Opportunity (EEO) guidelines for employers. Many states also have Civil Rights regulations which can be more restrictive than the Federal guidelines. In the case of hiring domestic employees (such as nannies, housekeepers, gardeners, etc.) the guidelines tend to be less stringent. However, you should be aware of your civil obligations.

All of the questions on the sample Employment Application are acceptable to ask a candidate for a nanny position. For example, child abuse is a very personal topic. However, in the case of a nanny, previous instances of abuse can be considered with respect to her ability to provide for your child's safety and health. The same applies for alcohol use, her health, and any criminal background.

If a candidate asks about this information, explain that it is within your legal rights as an employer because the information directly relates to her ability to perform the job.   If you are interested in additional details on this topic, contact your state Civil Rights office.

You may want to consider getting a copy of her driving record and performing a criminal record check.   Check with your state Deparment of Motor Vehicle to determine if you can get a copy of her   driving record directly, or if you must request it from her. Many states provide some form of criminal background information without a person's knowledge or permission.   This type of search applies to information on the public record, including previous arrests.   Contact your local police station to determine how and where to check criminal data.

A final option is to employ an investigation agency to check into the candiate's background more extensively.   There are agencies who specialize in this work, however the cost, timing, and service varies tremendously. Like anything else, the best source for such an agency is a reference from someone you trust and respect.

Remember, this person will be responsible for the most precious person in your life: your child.   You can never have enough information or be too careful.   If you are uncomfortable asking questions or obtaining information think about the incredibly unlikely but unfortunate situation in which something bad happens that could have been avoided with careful screening during your selection process.   Gather all the information you can, listen carefully for any clues, and make a well informed selection.

EMPLOYMENT APPLICATION
Live-Out Nanny

Name: _____   Phone: _____

Address: _____

City: _____   State: _____   Zip: _____

Date of Birth: _____   Age: _____   Social Security # _____

How long at current address? _____   If less than 2 years, list
previous address:
Address: _____
City: _____   State: _____   Zip: _____

Drivers License #: _____   License Plate #: _____
Make/Model of Car: _____   Insurance Company: _____
Do you have any tickets or accidents on your driving record?
Yes _____   No _____

	Attended?		Graduated?	
Grammar School	Yes ____	No ____	Yes ____	No ___
High School	Yes ____	No ____	Yes ____	No ___
College	Yes ____	No ____	Yes ____	No ___

If you graduated from college, what is your degree? _____
If you have a child care degree or training, please explain in detail:
_____
_____
_____

EMPLOYMENT APPLICATION

Employment History:

From/To	Job Description	Reason for Leaving
_____	_____	_____
	_____	_____
_____	_____	_____
	_____	_____
_____	_____	_____
	_____	_____
_____	_____	_____
	_____	_____

Do you have children of your own or by marriage? Yes   No ____
     If so, please list names and ages:

_____

_____

_____

_____

Are you CPR certified?   Yes _____   No _____
Do you smoke?   Yes _____   No _____
Do you have any health problems
     which could interfere with your
     ability to be a nanny?   Yes _____   No _____
Have you ever been arrested or
     charged for a crime?   Yes _____   No _____
Are you a recovering alcoholic?   Yes _____   No _____
Have you ever been abused?   Yes _____   No _____
Have you ever abused a child?   Yes _____   No _____

Please include any additional information which you feel should be considered with your application for a nanny position:

_____
_____
_____
_____
_____
_____
_____
_____
_____
_____

Please list a contact to be reached in the event of an emergency:

Name: _____   Phone #: _____

I attest that all of the above information is true.

Signed: _____   Dated: _____

Extending An Offer

Now that you have completed the interview process, including any necessary follow-up discussions with your candidate and her references, you are ready to make her an offer for the position.

You can extend the offer via the phone or in person, but you should document all of the details in writing. Give her a letter that describes your employment arrangements, including:

- salary (hourly or salary, and amount)
- start date (include any time she must set aside for orientation prior to starting full time)
- evaluation or probation period
- schedule (indicate how personal time, vacations, and holidays will be handled)
- benefits
- tax withholding status
- any special commitments or agreements

It's worthwhile to highlight the value of an evaluation or probation period at this point. This is a specific amount of time (one or two months, for example) after which either of you can cancel the arrangement if it's not working out. In the unfortunate event that a termination is necessary, it is much easier for everyone if this possibility has been addressed when she accepts the position.

While a formal probation period provides the best opportunity to evaluate her actual performance and your working relationship, some parents are able to set up a full or half-day arrangement with a preferred candidate to evaluate her *prior* to extending an offer.

This is most effective when someone (a parent, family member, or even an outgoing nanny) is at home to observe the candidate.

You can use either approach, or both, depending on your circumstance, to assess a candidate's capabilities and your level of comfort with her. What is important is to clearly establish the 'probationary' nature of this time regardless of when it happens and how long it lasts.

Following is a sample offer letter, which covers an evaluation period.

In addition to the offer letter, give her a copy of your Job Description including any modifications you have made as a result of your discussions. Together these documents will serve as your Work Agreement. She should review these documents and acknowledge her agreement by signing them prior to her first day.

The Work Agreement establishes an objective, mutual foundation for a successful relationship. It also offers you protection in the unfortunate event there is a disagreement about the nanny's responsibilities in the future. *Now* is the ideal time to get everything in writing even though it may feel formal and unnecessary. If you wait until later, you can end up with hurt feelings and a sense of lost trust — valuable aspects of your relationship you don't want to threaten.

November 1, 1993

Dear Mary:

We are pleased to extend this offer to you for a full time, live-out nanny position. You will be responsible for the care of our three-month-old son, Matthew.

Schedule: You will be expected to arrive at our home at 7:30 am and work until 5:30 pm, Monday through Friday. This schedule may vary occasionally; however you will be notified prior to any changes.

Wages: You will be paid on a hourly basis at $ 5.00 per hour. Any time over ten hours in a single day will be paid for at an overtime rate of $ 7.00 per hour. A quarter hour (15 minutes) will be smallest unit of time used to calculate wages. You can expect a paycheck on the 15th and 30th of the month. If these days fall on a weekend, you'll receive your check on the Friday prior.

Status: You will work as our employee, and at your request, we will withhold taxes. Additionally, we will assume responsibility for tax payments, social security, Medicare, and so on, as required by State and Federal law. We require the completion of W4 and I9 forms prior to or on your start date.

Vacation: You will be entitled to one half-day (five hours) paid vacation per month. You can accumulate this time and take no more than five consecutive days off. We require a minimum of one week advance notification of vacation time.

OFFER LETTER

Holidays: You will receive the following holidays as paid time off (one day equals ten hours pay): July 4th, Thanksgiving, and Christmas.

Start Date: We wish to set a start date no later than November 10th. We would like to have a half day orientation, for which you will be paid, sometime before you begin full time. The first two months will be considered an evaluation period. Although we anticipate a successful arrangement, this period is intended to help everyone adjust. If for any reason, the arrangement is not acceptable, you will be paid through your last day of work and released from your obligations.

Other: The Job Description which you have had the opportunity to review and discuss, includes the specific duties and responsibilities for this position.

We are impressed by your qualifications and enthusiasm and believe that Matthew will benefit from your care. Please do not hesitate to call if you have any further questions. We look forward to your acceptance.

Sincerely,

Diane Keefe

I agree to the conditions and requirements as outlined in this letter and the attached Job Description. A signed copy of this letter, and the Job Description, constitute our Work Agreement.

Nanny: _____ Date: _____

MANAGE WITH CARE

The time and energy you've invested in finding a nanny will provide many benefits once you are working together. You and your nanny will share a clear understanding of her role and how you will interact together. You will feel comfortable in her ability to integrate well with your family, and confident that you will achieve the kind and quality of child care you desire.

This section reviews some issues and recommends some activities to assist in establishing and maintaining a productive relationship with your nanny.

Getting Started

An orientation session is a good first step. With the pressure of interviewing removed, all of you can relax, get to know each other, and get down to the practicalities of the job. Everyone in the family should be encouraged to participate in the orientation if possible — especially your child if he's old enough. Here is a list of topics to review and things to do during the orientation:

- Tell her about special toys, treasures, habits or places that are important to your child.

- Talk through a typical day's routine and point out any possible variations or exceptions. Discuss your child's daily habits, especially with respect to dressing, bathing, and of course diapers (or bathroom).

- Tell her about your child's interests and abilities. Let her know what his skill sets are. He may be only five-months old but he can crawl with the best of them! Or, your four-year old loves to bake. Also, talk with your nanny about your child's fears or things which make him upset. For example, Monday mornings are often harder than others because of all the special time spent with Mom and Dad over the weekend.

- Show her around the house and explain what is considered 'community' property or areas, versus 'private'. For example, she is welcome to use the exercise bike, but the antique book collection is off limits. Set aside some space for her — a shelf, closet, room depending on your home — where she can keep personal belongings.

- Explain any appliances (washer/dryer, microwave, air conditioning, heat, vacuum cleaner) or systems (security, television, stereo) she will need to use. Again, point out anything that is not available to her or your child.

- Go through the pantry and kitchen, pointing out special items or favorite utensils ("Matthew only drinks milk out of his Batman cup"!)

- Show her the first aid kit and fire extinguishers. If you don't have them — get them.

- Let her know about any personal or family pet peeves she will be happy to avoid.

- Introduce her to neighbors to welcome her to the neighborhood. This smoothes the way for everyone in the event of a minor or major emergency.

• Discuss how you want her to handle unexpected events in her day. For example, you may require that she does not open the door to a stranger unless you have given her advance notice of an expected visitor. This means she ignores people delivering packages, fertilizing the lawn, or anyone else claiming to have a legitimate purpose in your home. This may create some minor inconveniences for you, but it absolutely eliminates the possibility of an unwelcome or potentially harmful visitor in your home.

• Take a picture of your new nanny. It is fun for your child, but more importantly, it is additional information about her which could be helpful in some unforeseen future circumstance.

Here is some helpful information you can compile for her:

• Write a list of contacts including phone numbers for both parents' office, neighbors, pediatrician, poison control, and emergency (fire, police, medic). This should be easy to find around *all* phones.

• Set up a list of preferred or 'approved' foods for breakfast, lunch, and dinner.

• Set up a written log where she can record daily events, including meals eaten (when, what, how much), naps taken, dirty diapers made (or not made!) and other activities of interest. This is extremely useful in helping parents stay in tune with their child's habits and development.

• Write down any instructions relating to medication for your child. You should *always* put this information in writing. Don't rely on your nanny's memory for dosage or timing.

Finally, here is something you should do for yourself as soon as you get your nanny settled in: line up a back-up nanny or baby-sitter. Although the thought of yet another extensive search so soon sounds very discouraging, do yourself a big favor and get it done now.

The reasons for a back up sitter are very simple. First, you know your nanny will at the very least take vacation days. She is also a human being so she may get sick or have unanticipated family demands. If you take the time now to find a temporary person you are comfortable with, it will significantly reduce the temporary upset caused by your nanny's absence. In addition to saving yourself the frenzy of a last minute search, you may save yourself some money. Fast and convenient temporary replacements tend to be more costly than someone you have previously worked with.

You will also benefit from the opportunity to get familiar with your back-up by having her baby-sit one night, or at the very least come over and meet with you and your child *before* you need her.

Finally, this search doesn't have to be extensive or involved. It may not even be a search at all.   Perhaps you have a friend or relative who can help out if you have discussed the arrangements ahead of time.

If none of the above convinces you, consider the following corollary to Murphy's Law: Your nanny will always have a family emergency the Sunday night prior to the day of your big presentation, for which you must catch a plane at dawn, which is the same day your spouse has a new job interview, and which is the night your child comes down with a fever.

Talk, Talk, Talk!

Make time on a regular basis to talk with your nanny about your child's care. It will be easier to have informal discussions than to have formal 'reviews' however both are very important to you.

Set aside time within your daily routine to talk with your nanny about your child's day. Be on the lookout for any trends with your child, you, or his nanny which might indicate a problem or concern. The sooner you discover and talk about problems, the easier it is to fix them. Also, if you don't feel informed about your child and his daily routine, you might miss an opportunity for helping him.

For example, you are perplexed to find that your six-month-old is suddenly very restless and cranky during his evening walk — something you especially look forward to. After trying several different options without any luck, you happen to mention it to your nanny. It turns out she's been taking him for a walk every afternoon, which he loves, but it's apparent his limit is one walk a day. Now that you've uncovered the whole picture, you and your nanny can decide on the best way to handle things.

In addition to your daily informal sessions, you should set up a schedule of regular reviews. In the early stages of working with your nanny, these can be effective to have every other week. Every two weeks gives you both time to get a feel for needed changes and still review your progress within a reasonable time. Once you have settled into a routine, an occasional talk about 'how things are going' will accomplish several things:

- It gets you away from the day to day issues and lets you anticipate upcoming events or phases in your child's life.

> *"Well, Mary, we're thinking about starting to potty train when he turns two next month. Do you feel he'll be ready? Good. Here is how we'd like to approach it ...."*

- It creates an open forum to talk about how you can better handle situations.

> *"Next time you feel that Matthew is getting sick, go ahead and call us at the office right away. We would rather be interrupted, even if it's a false alarm, than run the risk of another emergency room visit!"*

Growing Pains And Gains

It is important to recognize your priorities and requirements will change as your child grows, your parenting style matures, and your family changes (more children for example). Your child care preferences may also be affected as you gain experience in working with your nanny. Regardless of the source or reason for change, you *must* take time to evaluate the significance of a new priority and incorporate it into your child's care accordingly.

Open communication remains the key which enables you and your nanny to adapt for these changes. Your regularly scheduled discussions are the best time to review issues and to make plans for addressing them. Sometime, you may solicit input from your nanny before you make a decision on an issue. Other times, especially if it has a major affect on her, you may present your decision directly. To sum it up — in some instances you'll welcome her input, while in others you won't.

The different dimensions of your position — employer, parent, and family member — often require different styles of communication. In every role you should always be direct and sensitive. Finally, nothing can get too complicated as long as your top priority remains your child's welfare.

As an *employer*, you will want to evaluate her performance and provide feedback to ensure she meets the job requirements. Consider an instance where you are very pleased with her work except she is regularly tardy. Your best approach is to:

- Focus on the unacceptable behavior.

    *"Mary I'd like to discuss your work
    schedule. We need you to be here at
    7:30 sharp. In the last week you've
    arrived almost 15 minutes later
    three separate days".*

- Explain why it is unacceptable and how it affects you or your child.

    *"When you come in late, it creates
    unnecessary confusion and tension
    for Matthew. I end up having to
    dash out the door feeling
    disappointed that both my day and
    his got off to a bad start."*

- Discuss how and when you expect it to be corrected. Perhaps she has underestimated the commute during rush hour traffic and it's a simple case of getting an earlier start. Be sure you gain her agreement on the corrective steps to be taken and when they should be accomplished.

As a *parent* you will tend to be vulnerable to those issues which are emotional or subjective rather than objective. These can range from minor things (you don't like the way she brushes his hair) to more important things (she is enforcing too many 'time-outs'). You may find that her ideas on these issues differ from yours. You may change your mind as a result of her insights.

Many parents make the mistake of overlooking the first or second indication of a problem with their nanny. This is due to the inevitable conflict in your role as both employer and parent. Consider the previous example of tardiness. You want to correct the problem but you cringe at the thought of leaving an angry nanny in charge of your child. It *is* difficult and most parents will adjust their tolerance level for infractions based on this very real emotional reaction. However, if you have regular discussions and address infractions as soon as possible, you will minimize this uncomfortable conflict.

What is important during these discussions is the emphasis you place on doing what's best for your child. Talk to her with this in mind, and together you will create a positive environment within which to reinforce your priorities. If you find yourself in a gentle (or not so gentle) tug of war with your nanny over child care issues, never forget that *you* ultimately set all the rules. Do not hesitate to remind her that while you value her judgment she must accept your decisions in all cases.

The last dimension of your role has to do your nanny as a *family member*. A nanny will integrate with different families to different degrees. Whether you get very close or remain more distant, the mere fact that she is in your house everyday, all day long, can create opportunities for difficulty in your relationship.

The most common problem occurs when parents feel that their nanny is overstepping her bounds or taking advantage of her role. It can be small annoyances or large impositions; and it may or may not have anything to do with your child. It's the same phenomenon that occurs with visiting relatives who you may love dearly, but who can out stay their welcome.

If you become uncomfortable with her in this manner, deal with it directly and quickly. As always, it's best to address her behavior rather than her personally, and avoid making judgments. You are entitled to your unique family preferences but that doesn't mean you are right and she is wrong. Respect for her as a person with genuine feelings and preferences, combined with common courtesy, will also help get these issues resolved with a minimum of hurt feelings.

The ideal way to maintain quality child care in your home is to find a nanny who truly loves children and her job. Your full involvement and commitment in hiring and working with your nanny will encourage a loving relationship between her and your child, and promote a positive work experience for her.

CHANGES FOR THE BETTER

Most parents feel the experience of hiring and working with a nanny is very worthwhile. In addition to achieving your goals for quality care, you will also gain many insights to your child, your family, and yourself as a parent. Often, it is these very insights which will prompt you to consider changes in your child care priorities.

Do not despair if your new priorities don't include your current nanny, or any nanny at all. As with the other aspects of child care discussed in this Guide, commitment to your child's welfare and careful consideration of the issues will be your best approach to handling the change. Accordingly, this section presents issues to think about in the event you decide you no longer require your nanny's services.

When Family Priorities Change

Even if you are very happy with your nanny, it's possible that you will decide to let her go. You may decide that your toddler is ready for greater social interaction and would benefit from an

90

institutional day care arrangement or preschool. Your employment situation may change or require a move to a new location. Perhaps you decide to have another child and 'Mom' will take a few years off to stay home with the kids.

In these circumstances, you can minimize the impact of the change on everyone by keeping these things in mind:

- Be open about the reason for the change. Your nanny will be more than willing to assist in the transition if she clearly understands that it is not due to any failing on her part.

- Be clear about what and when will happen during the transition so she can plan accordingly. For example, if you are moving in three months, you may want to ask to for her commitment to remain during that time. In return, you can assist her in looking for another position by allowing time off for interviews and by providing a reference.

- Don't overlook the fact that she is losing more than a job. Most likely she has a very close relationship with your child, and has become an integral part of the family. You may want to encourage ongoing contact in the future, especially if this appeals to your child and fits with your new situation.

When Things Aren't Working Out

It is not uncommon for families to update their expectations as they gain experience actually working with a nanny. Responsibilities they thought were important are replaced by other responsibilities that weren't originally considered. As a result, you may have hired someone who really isn't qualified to do the job.

You may also find that your nanny isn't performing to your standards in spite of sincere efforts on your part to work with her.

Finally, there are those unfortunate circumstances where a failure on her part demands an immediate change.

Regardless of the cause, this can be a difficult situation for everyone. And unless the situation is very extreme, your child probably has an affection and comfort level for her which is difficult to break. You must also deal with the practical problem of replacing her.

Here are some recommendations to help you handle the change with a minimum of stress:

- Once you have made up your mind to make a change, move forward as quickly as possible. Every day that you keep your current nanny you will find new reasons to dislike her or to be worried. This is not an ideal situation for you or your child and it is likely she will eventually sense the problem and further compound things.

- The most effective way to proceed is with your 'employer' hat on. Assuming the role of employer will enable you to be fair and objective with her. It will also help you reduce the emotional distress, especially if you care for her as a person in spite of the cause of her dismissal.

- If you are unable to get interim child care while you look for a new nanny, it's best to conduct a search for a replacement before you dismiss her. This is not an attempt to deceive or mislead her in any way. It simply avoids the situation where you are without child care or where you are tempted to ask her to stay on until she can be replaced (*never* a good idea!). Remember, your top concern is for your child.

• Be prepared to explain the situation to your child on a level equal to his understanding. (However, talk with him *after* you have dismissed his nanny to avoid the possibility of him breaking the news to her instead of you!) If appropriate, reassure him that he hasn't done anything to make you send his nanny away.

There are a number of things you can do to make the dismissal discussion go smoothly:

• Have the discussion at the end of the day. Even if things go well, it is best not to have her come back — you could be putting your child at risk if she develops any resentment upon further reflection.

• She is entitled to an explanation but don't become defensive or overly apologetic. Focus your comments on her behavior or actions rather than on her personally. Emphasize that you have made the decision based on what you consider to be best for your child.

• Have a check made out to pay her wages through the last day. Depending on her length of service and the nature of the dismissal, you may want to include severance pay.

• If she has personal belongings that can be conveniently collected, let her do so. If it will take too long, tell her she can return at a specified time and pick them up.

• Do not include your child in the dismissal discussion — this could lead to an emotional, rather than objective situation. Do provide an opportunity for her to see him briefly if he is old enough to understand that she won't be coming back. Even if she is angry, it's important for him to have the chance to say good-bye.

It would be ideal if you found one perfect nanny and kept her for as long as you needed one.   Unfortunately, it's much more common for families to go through the process of hiring a nanny more than once. The adjustment to the absence of your old one and the pressure of finding a new one is compounded if your time frame is very short.   While this can be a stressful situation, remember: you found one once before and you'll do it again, and the change is for the better!

AFTERTHOUGHTS

A wise person once said: Becoming a parent is simultaneously the best and the worst thing that can happen to you. This person probably said this after a long, sleepless night with her colicky newborn. Just when this person was overcome with exhaustion and frustration, ready to scream or cry or do both, she gazed down at her unexpectedly silent child — a child now sleeping contentedly in her arms, the very picture of an angel from heaven.

"How many times", she wondered, *"will I ride this roller coaster of hopeless frustration to heart-melting awe? Maybe,"* she yawns, *"when he starts sleeping through the night ... "*

Another wiser person has said: It's a life long ride honey, so strap yourself in tight and don't close your eyes at the scary parts!

No other role in life compares to your role as a parent. And no other person can fill your shoes. You are the parent when you are at work each day. You are the parent when you go on a business trip. You are the parent when your child is embarrassed by the fact that you are the parent. You are the parent when college tuition comes due. You are still the parent, when after five years of college for a four year degree, your child returns home to live with you while looking for work (for the next five years).

So congratulations! You are a parent! Will you have occasional pangs of guilt about your choices? Probably. Will you make mistakes? Guaranteed. Will you ever do all the things for your child you think you should do? Nope. Are these questions unique to parents using nannies? Absolutely not! These concerns come with the job and are expressed by all parents, with or without nannies.

These afterthoughts really fall into the category of Perspective, or keeping the 'big picture' in sight. Remembering the 'big picture' (especially when the 'little picture' tends to get overwhelming) is very helpful for parents who have chosen to hire a nanny for their child.

So now you know the formula. It's quite simple: understand your family's priorities, make decisions according to your child's best interests, and keep your best perspective on hand at all times. Oh! almost forgot …   tell your friends you learned it all here in *HOW TO HIRE A NANNY!* Best of luck!